Midnight Passions

Here in the dark

Next to your heat

I feel the warmth within you

I hear your heartbeat

I hear the soft sounds that escape your lips

The anxious movement of your hips

The swelling pearl you hide within

The gasping moans when I am in

The rising of your breasts

As you take your next tortured breath

I relish the softness of your skin

The passion that resides deep within

I love the layers of sweat

That stains the sheets

The way your eyes lock into mine

Like it will never end

No passage of time

Forever I hold you in my arms

Locked in erotic bliss

Your body becomes mine at midnight

Your soul at the first kiss

The day before the first day

On the eve

Before that glorious day

The words came to me

I knew what to say

As I waited for you

To walk down the aisle

Your beauty, your happiness

Caused me to smile

And know the decision

That we were about to make

Was a lifelong commitment

That together we would partake

And with the vows

And the ring and a kiss

Not a moment of life

Would I ever miss

For with that moment

The locking of souls

The journey had begun

No matter where we go

And now here is what I must say

I will love you forever

For all of my days

Waves

Gently the water laps the shore

All of eternity, forevermore

Pressing softly in the sand

Simple caress of liquid hand

Rolling over seashore fauna

Intersecting with one another

Over and over the coming tide

Backwards and forwards nowhere to hide

Crushing blow to delicate touch

Infinite variables changes much

Staring into the quiet sea

A time of bliss and tranquility

This is all it will ever be

As wave after wave washes over me

December Interlude

Morning mist, winter's hand

Barren trees, empty land

Covered ground filled with snow

Arctic freeze, nothing will grow

Frigid wind blows straight through the bones

Empty buildings creak and moan

Withered life with no rules to adhere

No longer sustained, cannot endure

In the caves and under the trees

Wildlife slumbers, life sleeps

Awaiting for that special day

The first warmth of the sun's rays

To start the cycle once again

As winter passes and spring begins

Nobody People

I sit alone on a bench in this park

Been here all day, it has now turned to dark

Called out to the passerby's but my voice went unheard

Is it my dirty clothes? Or my ragged beard?

I wish I could change the way

I live my life everyday

But circumstances converged to decide my fate

How many days has it been since I last ate?

I lift up my tired bones

Walk the streets still alone

Wondering where it all went wrong

This information I do long

Maybe then I could make the change

My pathetic life would rearrange

Until then I wander this city

Under gazes of scorn and pity

The others contempt takes its' toll

As I am left a nobody with a tired soul

In the morning

Every morning she returns

See her loving gaze

That can make hearts burn

For many, many days

Teardrops fall from her eyes

Windswept is her hair

Helps to cover up the lies

As your drawn closer to her lair

The words that are spoken

Yet you do not begin to hear

The truth has been broken

That much is clear

Deception invades every space

And there is nowhere to go

Every morning she returns

The Goddess is awake

For that my soul yearns

Even when it is a mistake

Unspoken

Wind through the trees

Gentle rustling of the leaves

Like your name on my lips

I dare not speak

The soft caress of your fingers

Across my broken skin

The longing and desire

The endless sin

Waiting and wanting

Willing for your touch

Dying for the sound of your voice

Begging for your acceptance

Will I be the chosen one?

Will I win your heart?

Have I been good enough?

Or will you tear me apart?

Wicked Games

Flavor of the day

Special of the weak

The twisted games we play

Cannot be won by the meek

Silence speaks volumes

As does every glance

Just a step away from nothing

This is the only chance

Can we see eye to eye

Before that fateful day

The love finally dies

This journey is no longer fun

The prize has become the only goal

In this wicked game we play

Who will become the winner?

And have the final say

False Prophet

Bring me your weak

Your frail and your sick

Come forth the meek

Time to take your pick

From any desire you can choose

Swear off what you wish to lose

It is high time you made the choice

Let it be heard, your pathetic voice

Rise up from the struggles that keep you down

Turn that frown upside down

Fill your day infinite joy

Your nights with endless pleasure

Become the ultimate toy

The new greatest measure

And give to me my final goal

Relinquish to me your eternal soul

Only then will you realize as you take your last breath

That I am the false prophet

That led you to your death

Acid Rain on a Sunny Day

Take in your surroundings

See it with clear eyes

The misery and the pain

That joy that always dies

Look closer at the people

Surrounding you every day

Never a kind word to them

Do you say

Feel the sorrow, the empty existence

Look at your surroundings

Do you now begin to see?

The hollow feeling you feel

Is also the same for me

Where have all the bright lights gone?

Where is the joy?

Where is the sun?

Breathe in your surroundings

The stale air and the smell of fear

Hear every emotion as it begins to tear

The fabric of everything you thought you knew

And feel the rain as it falls on your face

Washing away the memories of this place

Needing You

A message received

From an unknown sender

A call for completion

And total surrender

Sight unseen

Voice unheard

Is this all a dream?

Or the beginning of something more

Am I your saint or your sinner?

Am I an angel or a devil?

Are my words the truth?

Or just peppered with lies

Will you recognize me?

When looked upon by your eyes

Every broken heart

Every shattered soul

Had someplace to start

Before life took its' toll

And now the road is forked

With many paths and choices

Each with their own needs

And distinct voices

The question becomes not what on each path lay

But where to start, to go which way

Every day the clock ticks

Closer we come to the time we die

And living unhappy is no life at all

Take my hand into a world of surprise

And let me guide you to where you cannot fall

With fulfillment and understanding

The rebirth of your damaged soul

And the start of this journey

Becomes the only way to go

Touched

Lying there naked

Underneath my gaze

The written words are upon you

Waiting for their say

Spellbound by my voice

The rhythm and tone

The remembrance of this night

Will carry you through when you are alone

The book still rests in the special crook

As my hands glide over your breasts

You close your eyes, dare not to look

As what to come will be the test

Concentrate on the words I speak

While I move slowly inside you

Bringing you closer to that peak

The sheen of sweat coats your skin

As I work myself deeper within

Hitting upon your very core

Until your ragged breath begs for more

All the while the book remains

Firmly in place no worry of stains

As I move quicker inside of you

This becomes what you most want to do

Fell the rising ebb and flow

As both my body and words

Fill your soul

Night Searcher

Bells toll in the distance

As I take flight

Wings outstretched I begin to glide

Into the dark and moonless night

Searching out my prey far and wide

Through the forest I quickly fly

Knowing before sunrise something will die

My piercing yellow eyes

Cast an evil glare

Throughout my kingdom I fly

Where nothing else can compare

Over the water I continue to soar

Still looking to complete my quest

This black starless night

Is truly a test

Before me now I spot my prey

Swooping down to where it lay

Do not shed a tear, do not cry

For my victim tonight had to die

In my grasp

I now have my feast

As I return to my lair

The king of the beasts

How people shake at the coming tide

Isn't it funny how people shake?

When the end is near

Isn't it funny how people shake?

When confronted with their fears

Isn't it sad to see people shake?

When there is no place to run

Isn't it terrible to see people shake?

When there is no more fun

Isn't it funny how people shake?

When everything they once loved is gone

And isn't it funny how people ache

When they realize it is done

Isn't it sad how people think?

That everything can be saved

Brought back from the brink

Isn't it tragic how people shake?

When it finally dawns

Isn't it funny how people shake?

When they realize they are nothing but pawns

?

Thoughts of a wandering soul

Silenced by the words

Unspoken, never said

Stopped from moving forward

By the impending dread

All the bridges never crossed

Paralyzed by fear

The shame and disgrace

Every time you are near

Held back by uncertainty

Giving up my goals

Frozen in time and taking its' toll

When the end is here

What will be the verdict?

Fulfilled potential

Or only life of conflict

Am I cursed to be nothing but failure?

In everyone's eyes

Have I been led down this path?

Only to die

?

Release me from this damnation

Before it is my time to go

Give me back my life

Give me back my soul

Step

This is the first step

Over the cliff

That has held me

Firmly in its grasp

I plunge through the air

Feeling the wind rush up towards me

I have escaped

I am now free

Floating downward balance by the air

Whether I even land I do not care

My heart beats like a drum

My ears filled with a thump

The whistling of the air

Forms a pocket around me

From this freedom

Life I can now see

From this cliff

I have stepped

Into the stars in the sky

Out of the abyss

I have taken the very first step

And I did not fall

I can take more steps

I can take them all

I am released from the prison

That held me back

Loosed from the shackles

I can now attack

Life at its fullest

And no longer ask what if

I never took that very first step

Plague Bearer

My plague

Infects your every pore

Leaving you breathless

Begging for more

Changing your cells

More to my liking

Beginning of your hell

As your body starts dying

Feel the difference a moment makes

The mutation of my plague is all it takes

You no longer are yourself

Your mind becomes mine

No amount of begging or wealth

Will change the outcome this time

My plague has infected you

Taken your very soul

You have no choice

You have lost all control

Know that my love for you is true

My plague is my gift to you

Succumb to my twisted will

Bite into that bitter pill

No longer will you even have to feel

My plague is the ultimate prize

Feel the infection this is what is real

As your soul dies

Until the end of time

When I can then dine

Erasure

Feels so cold now

Like I am being erased

Feels so alone now

After I was replaced

No one can save me

From the path that lie ahead

Filled with darkness

The souls of the dead

Crowd around for a chance

To grasp at my being

Take back with you a bit of light

Bring themselve's happiness for a moment

As I am drawn further into the night

Feels so cold now

Like this is a mistake

What did I do to deserve this?

Why in me did you forsake?

Can I send you a transmission?

Will my scream be heard?

Is this life in remission?

Can the sickness be cured?

Cut the strings that bind me

Find me a room

To escape the loneliness

The blackness and gloom

Let me sleep tonight

With your powerful might

You have become the only person

To end this wretched perversion

New Scourge

From the ashes of her tainted love

Rose a single bloom

Born from the blood of her blackened heart

Brightness amongst the gloom

Sharpened talons ripped away the flesh

Destroyed to the bone

Time to start fresh

Already alone

Darkness fades into morning light

The spirit had been reborn

The finality of endless night

Forever been scorned

Rising now from the ground

A new form emerges

A with a screeching sound

The arrival of a new scourge

Jealous

I am the wretched spawn

Born from the twisted union between love and hate

My appetite you can never sate

I feed on the fear

The end of everything you hold dear

I am the look of disgust in your eyes

Not believing the truth, only the lies

I am the misunderstanding of simple gestures

The forgotten words and the endless lectures

I am the cold shoulder to your touch

The flinching movement when it becomes too much

I am the stolen glances across the room

The intuition that it will end soon

My birth is foretold in misery

My reach extends in the life of everybody

I am the last emotion before the love dies

And the hate truly begins

The middle ground is where I fester and bloom

A green eyed monster ready to be groomed

The Start

With a heavy heart

And saddened eyes

I move aside

As the love dies

No more tears no more threats

No more fears no more regrets

Standing alone once again

A position I have been in before

To once more begin

Searching for a new door

To open up and be surprised

The heartfelt laughs galore

The happy loving cries

To once again find the joy

That has evaded me for so long

To be overwhelmed by that glorious song

And hear the words that once rang true

The tender caress of "I love you"

Symphonic destruction

With dark passion

Play the strings to my heart

With repercussion

Destroy it part by part

Slide your fingers through my flesh

There is no stopping the symphony

As together we mesh

And then the epiphany dawns upon your cold eyes

The music to your ears

Was the sound my soul makes as it dies

And suddenly you feel the fears

For without my life force to keep you sated

Then you will have nothing left to hold on to

As if this was preordained or fated

Your essence becomes unglued

Once the strings are plucked one by one

And I have lost every part of my soul

Your magic orchestra will be done

And you will have no place to go

Permissive Eroticism

Sweat soaked skin

Glimmering in the moonlight

My gentle touch

The first of the night

My fingers glide over your thigh

Gentle pressure gives way to pleasure

And your contented sighs

Become my treasure

The soft caress as I continue to travel

Across your body with my nails

Your composure starts to unravel

As your resistance fails

The tension is mounting

My fingers moving quicker

You begin counting

Like the last seconds of a bomb ticker

The sensation enfolds you

Your breathing is out of control

No way to hide what you will do

As the passion explodes

I remove my fingers

From where they were hidden

And with a soft slow touch

Once again I begin

Ravishment

Upon my lips the taste of you

The essence of life which I drink

The sweet nectar that is true

To bring me to the brink

The swirl of my tongue within the folds

Wetness so pure

The ecstasy of the moment untold

The agony you must endure

From your body I quench my thirst

Bringing us both to the peak

You are far from the first

But the others we do not speak

This moment there is only one

From whom I must feast

Until the second you done

And love the feel of the beast

Unwanted Birth

Form the moment I was on this earth

The untold fear began to bloom

The trepidation of my birth

Held a lifetime of gloom

My presence to you has become a curse

No matter what I do or say

My very existence makes it worse

Each and every day

The misery began when I took my first breath

But who could have for seen

That the festering destruction would last until my death

Until there is no more hope to glean

My words you do not want to hear

My actions you scorn

My presence you do not want near

As your eyes wish I had never been born

Pulse

The touch of your fingers

On my skin

The sensation lingers

The start of sin

Your heat burns through my flesh

Through muscle and bone

My thoughts begin to mesh

Taking on a new tone

Electric pulses from your tongue

Drive me closer to the brink

My will had come undone

No longer can I think

Closer now I feel your presence

The time to act had come

Accepting your essence

We become one

Guerrilla warfare

Dead by dawn

We shall see

Fateful words spoken

In err to me

Through the fog and the gloom

Through the misery and the doom

The army marches closer now

To try and seal my fate

Take from me my living breath

Only If I placate

The night air is cold

From the forest not a sound

Silent I move into position

Close to the ground

The first glimpse of sunlight

I stifle my yawn

Though many have tried

I am still alive at dawn

Swept

With a gentle touch

Blossoms new found desire

The soft spoken words

Which ignite the fire

The quick glance to get attention

The first quick steps of newly discovered passion

The wanting hugs

The needy kissing

When not together

The time spent missing

The longing for each moment spent

The discovery of two

The appreciation I get

When I look at you

Kiss me with your fingers

Touch me with your eyes

Ecstasy that lingers

True devotion never dies

Friendless

Glide into the oblivion of your own making

Burn every bridge. Never giving, always taking

Join with others

Celebrate with glee

As you undertake your festival

Of everything is about 'me'

Don't look as life passes you by

Never notice when people up and leave

Don't worry about anything

Until nothing is left to grieve

Is this the happiness you seek?

Where no one can tell you where to stand

Is this the joy you thought it would be?

When no one is there to lend a hand

Now this is the path you walk

The choices have been made

Your all alone now, people talk

The debts now need to be paid

Until the last time

The final straw

Still alone

Until your breath takes its' last draw

Last Moment

Will our sins be forgiven?

How will we be received?

If the way we lived are lives

Was while being deceived

Can we get redemption?

Pass the pearly gates

Or are we doomed to the pits of fire

Consumed by eternal hate

The path we walk is not always by choice

In our final talk will we have a voice?

Is the good we have done?

Weighed against the wrong

Or is it just the sins we have committed

That is looked upon

Can we hope for forgiveness?

When so hard to understand

Will we be forgiven?

Will you hold out your hand?

The Longing

Can you hear my voice?

Whispering soft goodnights

Do you feel my touch?

At morning's first light

Do you still remember that very first sight?

Or how I thought of you alone at night

Can you recall the spoken words?

That made you feel

Or the gestures from me to help you heal

Close your eyes once again, hear the sound

Of my voice within your head

Listen to what I say, there are no bounds

Take my hands, let yourself be led

Feel the passion glide across your skin

The beating of my heart

Know that there is no sin

But the space that keeps us apart

I wish again to hold you

Keep you close to me

Place a kiss upon your lips

And set your soul free

Darkness of a brightened heart

Bittersweet the moment you were gone

Hardly had started before it was done

And know I wonder what I did wrong

To make you so quickly move along

My words I gave you from the heart

The first connection was a good start

And as quickly as the time passed

Realized somehow that this would not last

A part of me saddens at the thought

Feel as If I was never really given a chance

To prove that what we had was right

Not just a stolen glance

So quietly I exit from your life

I will not shed a tear

For even though love cuts through you like a knife

I am no worse for the wear

I will miss the sound of your voice

The thought of what could have been

And even though I had no choice

I hope one day to meet again

Trees

Splintered from the tree of life

A tiny sliver

Filled with pain and strife

The very thought makes you quiver

From the thought and the fear

That this little piece

Can end everything you hold dear

On the branches of the tree of wisdom

Holds the truth

Of beauty and reason

From this tree it becomes so clear

That love can conquer

And make good what you hold dear

Deep in the roots of the tree of Hate

Lies the horrors

That only evil can appreciate

And in this tainted soil

Where misery festers and grows

No one can ever bear

To hold onto anything that is dear

Within each person

A piece of each tree exists

Giving instruction

Which to persist

And only the person is in control

On which tree is allowed to grow.

Quiet Passion

Quiet passion

Built on lies

Empty promises

And alibis

Soft spoken words

Which hold no truth

Brutal reality

When it is up to you

Calm and twisted

Filled with pain

Black hearts filled

Again and again

Angry shouts

And bitter glances

Wretched life

With no advances

Darkened soul

Black as night

Filled with rage

But that's alright

With piercing eyes

Called to action

The start again

Of this quiet passion

The passing

The sorrow I feel at the passing

Of something I thought was everlasting

Start fresh and anew

Find a soul to escape the gloom

Release the scream

Lodged in my throat

Live life, not the dream

Tear down the fetid moat

That surrounds my heart

No longer an ending

But a start

Flush the salt

From my wounds

Find the faults

Amongst the doom

Rinse the pain

Cleanse my eyes

Stop the torture

Stop the lies

End the charade

Cease the fall

Your life on parade

This is your call

The time is now

It is alright

Close the eyes

With a kiss and good night

Long Dark Walk on a Sunlit Path

With a silence I walk alone

Staring at the trees

Listening to the sounds around

All laughing at me

Walking down the winding path

Wonderment abound

Glistening sunlight invades

The soft tortured ground

A tunnel approaches

The blackness I enter

Shielded from the light

My soul I surrender

In the darkness

I find my place

A comfortable zone

Of darkened grace

The stillness likened to a tomb

Lightless but with no fear

Wandering aimlessly in the gloom

Nothing sacred, nothing dear

All to soon the darkness fades

And the path lights up again

With the brilliance of sunlight

Blocking out where you have been

I stare down the well worn path

With its' splendor beckoning

I turn back towards the darkness

To let it envelope me once again

Shining Moments

Sparkling like moonlight

Across the sea

Your beautiful smile

At the sight of me

Your open arms

The gentle touch

The soft caress

That becomes too much

My open heart

For all to see

Left undone

What shall be

With softened lips

Passions kiss

Beating hearts

And unending bliss

Walking away

Without a sound

Try another day

Meet on common ground

The shining moments

Never seem to last

Until one day

They are all in the past

Poison Arrows

How do I escape Cupid's poison?

A constant reminder of where I have been

Keeping the pain very fresh

Of all the people with I did not mesh

Seeping into every pore

Poisons damage keeping score

My beating heart begins to bleed

With the semblance of want and need

I long again for your touch

This waiting game has become too much

Cupid's arrow long and true

Did it make a mistake when it hit you?

The eyes have seen, the mouth has spoken

The ears have heard, nothing is broken

Yet in your haste to deny your love

Forgotten the meaning from above

Chances few, should never be forsaken

Or one day your true love will have been taken

So here I sit, here I wait

Maybe one day you will appreciate

And I hope that when I have become the one

Cupid's love has not gone

Devotion and desire

Devotion and desire

Bitter words to every liar

No room for love amongst deceit

Every moment another defeat

Spoken words that have no meaning

Is the crux of their whole being

Poisoned motion the whole existence

From these people you keep your distance

Back into the arms that hold

If you are willing to be so bold

Devotion lacking without desire

Let me be the one to stoke the fires

Show you how life can be

When with someone just like me

The flames of passion burn brightly

And my love for you is shown nightly

From the gentle kiss

To the soft caress

The life with you

Is what I miss

Come back to where you felt the warmth

The tenderness of my soul

Together we are one

On the journey we will go

Your place in me

A precious jewel

Was revealed for all to see

The day dawned bright

When you found me

Wandering through misery and haze

My heart melted from your gaze

Your presence breathed life into my soul

And showed me just how far we could go

Your beauty radiates from within

Casting out and reeling me in

Your words are like water washing over my mind

Each day something new to find

To hold you each day is a pleasure

One of many hidden treasures

My heart beats to infinity

As I have now found my destiny

My love still grows with each days passing

And I know what I am missing

Take my hand let it begin

Let me be your strength as you are mine

We can once again walk hand in hand

And forget about time

Let me search into your eyes

You can do the same, there are no lies

Time has a way of making one forget

All that is good

Let us once again reunite

The way that we should

I reach out to you

Soul, body and mind

Know that I love you

Now and til the end of time

Runaway

Searching

I call out your name

My screams pierce the night

It is still the same

And things are not alright

Since the day you said goodbye

We still pretend it is okay

But we are both living a lie

The sun still rises

Even in different places

I search for you

Amongst all the faces

The fears were the same

Even if I never spoke them

No one is to blame

But nothing was broken

Seemed to soon you hit the panic switch

Stopping our time

Was this your true wish?

To not be mine

Eyes wide open I look

To find where you might be

My heart is what you took

When you ran away from me

Goodbyes and silent cries

When I said I loved you

That meant for all time

Not just for the moments

That you were mine

When I held you in my arms

Close to your heartbeat

You knew there would be no harm

My touch gentle and sweet

When I gazed into your eyes

Saw the joy mixed with the pain

I knew that I would die

If that ever happened to you again

When I took grasp of your hand

And squeezed it tight

I knew that I would love you

With all of my might

When I am alone

Gazing at the stars

I think of you

And you are never far

When I said I loved you

Not just any words to say

But what was heartfelt and true

On this my dying day

The Snowman Wept

The forest echoed with the now silent laughter

As icicles melted drip, drip, drip

From the branches and the rafters

Accelerating at a rapid clip

For the sun rose brightly

On that wintery day

A sky filled with brightest blue

No more clouds, no more grey

And at the edge of the forest in a yard

Created by a child a vision in white

Stood a snowman, his three round sections patted tight

A black hat and red scarf placed with care

Two eyes of black charcoal for which to stare

A golden nose and a bright candy smile

Created by a child from a snowy pile

And day after day that snowman stood

Always smiling as he should

But then the sun rose higher in the sky

And the snowman realized something was not right

His face had shifted like a tear from an eye

And the snowman began to struggle with all his might

To try and escape the brutality of the sun's glare

But all he could do is sit there and stare

Into the house where his dear child slept

Slowly melting the snowman wept

The Gift

A rose of rapture

And its' various hues

Empowered with beauty

As a gift given to you

Enjoyed by many

More than it seems

Have partook the gift by the light of moonbeams

And the stars that shine before your eyes tonight

Give truth to the beauty the gift holds

About the freedom given to do what they might

For the story is centuries old

But after all was done

The takers were all gone

Being mighty and bold

Using more than the rose's power could hold

And when the body is laid to rest

Then comes the true test

The beauty that was once so enthralling

In death becomes much more appalling

To this day the glory of the gift is ignored

Taken for granted like one is bored

Until the spell is finally broken

And the meaningful words are actually spoken

The power of the gift will remain abused

And the giver will be used

Until the day there is nothing left to offer

But an empty soul in the coffer

Can You

Can you stop the bleeding from this tattered heart?

Can you put back together the pieces you tore apart?

Can you look at me with the love you once had?

Can you admit to yourself that it was not all bad?

Tendrils of pain rip through my chest

As the blackness creeps further abreast

Sorrow fills my lungs taking away my every breath

The pain within know no depth

The misery invades my very mind taking its' toll

The darkness you laid upon me eats away my soul

My body still moves like a puppet on your string

Wondering which way to turn, what tomorrow will bring

Can you heal this sorry thing that was once so filled with life?

Can you end the tortures'? Put an end to the strife?

Will you welcome me with open arms, love filling my heart?

Or will you keep standing there tearing me apart?

The Final Sacrifice

Under the brightest of stars I was born

A beacon of hope to those who would hear

Happiness at my birth, but my future left many torn

As they did not know the tortures I would endure

And now on this day the journey must end

My teachings written down for all to believe

My will at this moment cannot bend

Or the winners will be those who deceive

The heavy wooden beams stand ready

The nails are sharp and new

Woven bindings in place to hold me steady

Nothing had been left askew

My tortured body is first prepared

Bathed in a vat of salt

So that the stinging whip blows are most feared

The beginning of the assault

I start my journey through the masses

Shamed with only a cloth

Nothing to protect me from their glances

The stones they throw are none too soft

I start up the path to the hill

To face my predetermined demise

I hear the demented laughter

I hear the anguished cries

Momentarily I lose my breath

From my side a sharp pain

I know soon will be my death

But at least there is something to gain

From my birth I knew the price

I knew what I was born to do

Commit the final sacrifice

Because of my love for you

□

Destroyed by your touch

Cut from my body this sacred part

Destroy from me my dying heart

Bleed out from me my will

From a thousand tiny wounds

Make sure that they never will heal

Bask in the glory of my destruction

Smile when I take my last gasping breath

Relish the fact that I did succumb

To your unholy love and a certain death

Take from me the very last reason

Starve from me any kind of affection

Lest not we forget to hide the joy

As I crumble down in front of you

A broken, ravished toy

Look not into my pained eyes

As the glimmer of hope fades away

Do not speak to me

As the words to kill me you want to say

□

Embark alone on your journey

My soul finally has been crushed

Wretched free from its' bindings

That once held it so near

Torn from my body

By your absolute hate and fear

Dissect my joy, happiness and laughter

Stomp on the dreams I once had

Look at the remains after

Kill off every piece of me

Drown it all away

Leave the corpse the way it was meant to be

To pick up and destroy once again another day

www.ingramcontent.com/pod-product-compliance
Ingram Content Group UK Ltd.
Pitfield, Milton Keynes, MK11 3LW, UK
UKHW041920190726
13854UKWH00003B/1353

9 780557 654574